THE ELECTION OF THE POPE

JIM CANTWELL

The Election of the Pope

ST PAULS

ST PAULS Publishing
187 Battersea Bridge Road, London SW11 3AS, UK
www.stpauls.ie

Copyright © Jim Cantwell 2002

ISBN 085439 641 1

Distributed in Australia and New Zealand by
ST PAULS PUBLICATIONS
P O Box 906, Strathfield NSW 2135, Australia

Set by TuKan DTP, Fareham, Hampshire
Printed by Interprint Ltd, Marsa, Malta

ST PAULS is an activity of the priests and brothers
of the Society of St Paul who proclaim the Gospel
through the media of social communication

Contents

Preface

In his most famous work, *Leviathan*, published in 1651, the English philosopher Thomas Hobbes dismissed the papacy as "not other than the ghost of the Roman Empire sitting crowned upon the grave thereof." Over 340 years later J.M. Roberts was to write in *The Penguin History of the Twentieth Century* (1999) that the papacy "sometimes seemed the most threatened of all religious institutions."

That the papacy survived the corruption, nepotism, greed, mismanagement and incompetence that periodically disfigured its features is, as a bishop humorously remarked to me, the most compelling proof of the existence of the Holy Spirit.

The history of the papacy traverses almost the entire landscape of human experience. The scandalous perversity of some popes is counterbalanced by the holiness and heroism of many more. The rashness and ignorance of the few is compensated by the wisdom and learning of the majority. Ruthlessness is mirrored by gentleness, negligence by vigilance, and rashness by prudence.

Many popes have been shaped and changed by the office itself. Some have found it an impossible burden while many others have discovered an inner strength they never knew they had. And some have added to the gaiety of their times by a flair for the absurd. Prospero Lambertini's (Benedict XIV's) biographer Caracciolo records that after his election he was once admonished for using the coarse colloquialisms of Bologna. He replied that he was now in a position to ennoble his native slang. When he had been Archbishop of Bologna, the Pope asked him to comment on complaints the Vatican had received about the Vicar-General of the diocese. It says much about Clement XII's humanity that he was mightily amused when Lambertini responded that he prayed daily to the divine Saviour "that He may be as content with His vicar on earth as I am with mine."

For many centuries the cardinals have elected the Pope in a secret ballot. The conclave is one of the oldest electoral assemblies in the world. When the cardinals meet behind the locked doors of the Sistine Chapel they will be reminded of the deceptively simple guiding principle laid down by Pope John Paul II in his Constitution for a papal election: "Having before their eyes God and the good of the Church they shall give their vote to the person…who in their judgement is most suited to govern the universal church in a fruitful and beneficial way."

It is the complex and fascinating process of seeking such that person that is the subject of this book.

Jim Cantwell
April 2002

1

The Bishop of Rome

A balmy autumnal warmth settles over Rome on the evening of 16 October 1978. The darkness is suddenly and brilliantly illuminated by television arc lamps beaming their powerful light onto the balcony of the Hall of Benedictions in the centre of the basilica overlooking St Peter's Square. The expectant crowd which had been in the square all day is boosted by many thousands more as the media broadcast the news that white smoke had begun to waft from the chimney of the Sistine Chapel at 6.15. The smoke from a fire of redundant ballot papers being burnt with dry straw announces to the world outside the Vatican Palace that a new pope has been elected.

The final act of a papal election is one of the most splendid pieces of theatre on earth. The doors to the loggia of the Hall of Benedictions open at 6.43 and the senior Cardinal-deacon steps out in front of the microphone. Cardinal Pericle Felice's deep and sonorous Latin echoes loudly around the Piazza: *Annuntio vobis gaudium magnum, habemus papam!* ('I announce to you a great joy, we have a pope!'). A mighty roar rises up, then gradually recedes into a diminuendo, providing the cardinal with a theatrical pause. He resumes: *Eminentissimum, Reverendissimum Dominum Cardinalem Carolum Woytyla qui sibi nomen imposuit Joannem Paulum Secundum* ('Most Eminent, Most Reverend Lord Cardinal Karol Woytyla, who has taken the name John Paul the Second').

"Chi è?" (Who is it?), the crowd murmurs in bewilderment. A loud voice shouts: *"È un straniero!"* The name certainly isn't Italian. *"Un Africano?"*, some ask. Assisting in a radio programme from the broadcasting booths of the Braccio Carlomagno, overlooking the square from its left, I hear astonished commentators emit gasps of disbelief. Some feel certain they misheard. "Voy-tee-wa...", one blurts out, incredulously, *"uno Polacco...* a Pole. Can it really be?" It was! Shortly after 'Papa Woytyla' appears on the balcony to give his first apostolic blessing *Urbi et Orbi* ('to the city and the world'). He surprises the throng by speaking excellent Italian and delights them by calling it *"la vostra lingua... la nostra lingua"* ('your language... our language').

Thus came to a truly astonishing end the second papal election within seven weeks. Albino Luciani, the Patriarch of Venice, had been elected Pope on 26 August. Like all of his predecessors since 1523, he was Italian. When he died suddenly 34 days later, there were few firm predictions about his successor except that he, too, was likely to be Italian. Few expected the cardinals to choose somebody from outside Italy for the first time in over 450 years. Still fewer expected that the new Pope would have come from beyond the Iron Curtain, from Poland, a country of enormous strategic importance to the Soviet bloc. At that time Moscow maintained a particularly oppressive hold on Poland through a puppet regime in Warsaw. In these circumstances, the election as the supreme leader of the Catholic Church of the Cardinal from Crakow was truly sensational. To some of the cardinals it may not have come as such a huge surprise because Woytyla had, in fact, received several votes in the first conclave of 1978.

The Archbishop of Crakow became the Bishop of Rome, one diocese among about 2500 in the Catholic Church. According to the *Annuario Pontificio*, the official international directory of the Catholic Church, it covers 881 square kilometres of the city and its environs, has 2.5 million Catholics in a general population of 2.6 million. It has 328 parishes and 723 churches served by 3,330 priests. Its statistical profile is similar to many large dioceses throughout the world. Rome differs significantly only in the large number of its churches and priests. But, in reality it is a diocese like no other in the Catholic Church. The Pope may be its bishop but the diocese of Rome is run on a day to day basis by a Vicar General, always a cardinal, and five auxiliary bishops. A team of officials administers the diocese from offices in the Lateran Palace, beside the basilica of St John Lateran, the pope's cathedral as Bishop of Rome.

However, soon after he became Pope John Paul II initiated a marathon programme of Sunday pastoral visits to all parishes of Rome diocese. These visits were preceded by intensive preparations involving priests and people of the parishes and the Pope himself. This initiative helped to restore in the minds of the Catholics of Rome a strong sense that the Pope is *their* bishop, *their* chief pastor. As the first non-Italian Bishop of Rome for over four centuries he was determined to show that not only did he speak "*la nostra lingua*" but that he was the leader of "*la nostra chiesa.*"

The last non-Italian Pope had been a Dutchman, Adrian VI, who was elected in 1522 but ruled for less than two years. He was the first pope to feel the full impact of the Reformation and to deal with the pressing need for reform in the Catholic Church. During the first millennium the vast majority of popes were born in Rome. The bishops attending the Third Lateran Council in 1179 were obviously pleased about this since they decreed that the choice of Pope should be made from within the Church in Rome. But it added an important rider, "if a suitable man could be found there"; if not, someone from a church outside Rome could be chosen. Being Roman was never a requirement for papal office. St Peter was not from Rome and his twelve immediate successors were all Greek speaking. While most of the popes in the first millennium were Romans, most in the second millennium were not. Relatively few native Romans have become popes in modern times. Pope Pius XII (1939-58) was the last to do so. Before him, one has to back over 200 years to find another, Innocent XIII (1721-24).

From earliest times the Bishop of Rome had much wider powers and responsibilities than the bishop of any other diocese. Christians from elsewhere looked to Rome for definitive guidance and advice for their particular churches. The authority of Rome grew as its bishops intervened in doctrinal disputes and suppressed heresies. Under Pope Leo I ('Leo the Great') in the fifth century Rome's influence was greatly expanded and consolidated because he articulated the conviction that the supremacy of his see had divine and scriptural authority. The authority of the pope is defined in Canon 321 of the Code of Canon Law: "The office uniquely committed by the Lord to Peter, the first of the Apostles, and to be transmitted to his successors, abides in the Bishop of the Church of Rome. He is the head of the College of Bishops, the Vicar of Christ, and the Pastor of the universal Church on earth. Consequently, by virtue of his office, he has supreme, full, immediate and universal ordinary power in the Church, and he can always freely exercise this power". In other words, the supreme authority of the pope is not a prerogative of honour but of substance.

The great second-century Bishop of Lyon, St Irenaeus, in his main work, *Against Heresies,* written during the pontificate of the twelfth pope, Eleutherus (AD 175-189), traced the succession of that Bishop of Rome back to Peter. Because they were in a direct line of succession from Peter, the Bishops of Rome had special authority within the Church. The First Vatican Council taught that the papacy was instituted by Jesus Christ's commission to Peter and was not the result of historical developments or even the intrinsic needs of the Church. The institution of the primacy of Peter "appears as a manifestation of Christ's concern for the inner unity and reliable proclamation of the message of salvation both within and without the people of God."[1] St Irenaeus wrote: "For every church must be in harmony with this Church (the church of Rome) because of its outstanding pre-eminence, that is, the faithful from everywhere, since the apostolic tradition is presented in it by those from everywhere."[2] An individual pope will obviously have his personal opinions on a whole range of matters but he is not entitled to impose them on others. When he acts as Pope, he does not do so as a private person but always as successor of St Peter. The defining characteristic of papal authority is one of service out of love. This is posited in the call that Christ gave to Simon in his three-pronged question, "Simon, Son of John, do you love me?" When Peter replied in the affirmative, Christ commanded him to "feed my lambs, feed my sheep" (Jn 21:15ff). Christ gave Simon a new name of powerful symbolic significance. He called him Peter (*Petros*, Rock, cf Mt 16:18-19).

Though the Pope has supreme authority he is not detached from the rest of the bishops of the Catholic Church, nor should his role be seen as resembling the chairman of an international conglomerate. The Primacy of the Pope is an essential focus of the unity of the Catholic Church. Canon 330 states: "Just as, by the decree of the Lord, Saint Peter and the rest of the Apostles form one college, so for a like reason the Roman Pontiff, the successor of Peter, and the bishops, the successor of the Apostles, are united together in one."

It is the direct link to the Apostle Peter that makes the See of Rome unique. The authority of the Pope cannot be transferred to others during his pontificate. He may and does delegate many functions and responsibilities to others. All of the offices of the central government of the Catholic Church – the congregations, councils, commissions and tribunals which constitute the Roman Curia, collectively known as dicasteries – have responsibility by delegation from the Pope for specific areas of the Church's work and mission. But they all operate under the Pope's authority and their functions cannot be detached from that authority. This becomes very clear during an interregnum in the papacy. When a pope dies the heads of all departments of the Roman Curia are suspended from the exercise of their authority – though their offices continue to function. A practical benefit of this arrangement is the freedom it gives the new pope to appoint his own "team" without causing any embarrassment to the previous incumbents. There are three exceptions:

1. the Vicar-General of Rome, for if his authority were suspended the diocese would be doubly-deprived of its leadership;

2. the Grand Penitentiary, who is responsible for matters relating to the Sacrament of Penance, because not even the death of a pope can cause confessional matters to be suspended;

3. the Cardinal-Chamberlain (Camerlengo) of the Holy Roman Church, because he is required to play a pivotal role in running the central government of the Church during the vacancy. He also organises the conclave to elect the new pope and presides over it.

2

The Vacant Chair

For many centuries popes have claimed the right and the freedom to determine the ground rules for managing the central government of the Church during a vacancy in the papacy and for the conduct of the papal election. In 1059, for example, Nicholas II asserted his "apostolic authority" to decree important changes in the election process. In 1975, Pope Paul VI's Constitution declared: "Down the centuries the Supreme Pontiffs have considered it their prerogative, and their right and duty, to determine in the manner considered best the election of their successors, opposing all tendencies that sought, through alterations in ecclesiastical institutions, to take away their exclusive right to decide upon composition of the body of electors and the latter's manner of exercising its functions."[3] More recently, Pope John Paul's Apostolic Constitution on the conduct of a papal election begins with these words: "The Shepherd of the Lord's whole flock is the Bishop of the Church of Rome, where the Blessed Apostle Peter, by sovereign disposition of divine Providence, offered to Christ the supreme witness of martyrdom by the shedding of blood. It is therefore understandable that the lawful apostolic succession in this See, with which 'because of its great pre-eminence every Church must agree' (St Irenaeus), has always been the object of particular attention." His Constitution affirms "an indisputable principle that the Roman Pontiff has the right to define and adapt to changing times the manner of designating the person called to assume the Petrine succession in the Roman See."[4] Its final paragraph states: "I lay down and prescribe these norms and I order that no one shall presume to contest the present Constitution and anything contained herein for any reason whatsoever. This Constitution is to be completely observed by all, notwithstanding any disposition to the contrary, even if worthy of special mention. It is to be fully and integrally implemented and is to serve as a guide for all to whom it refers... I hereby declare abrogated all constitutions and orders issued in this regard by the Roman Pontiffs, and at the same time I declare completely null and void anything done by any person, whatever his authority, knowingly or unknowingly, in any way contrary to this Constitution."

The norms governing the election of the pope were revised periodically in response to problems or anomalies that arose at particular times. Until the twentieth century the revisions tended to be piecemeal. Modern popes, however, have adopted a more systematic approach by issuing new constitutions. Pius X promulgated the first formal Constitution, *Vacante Sede Apostolica,* on Christmas

Day 1904. He was an extremely reluctant pope. He pleaded with the conclave in 1903 not to choose him and only consented to election after a marathon session of persuasion by several friends among the cardinals. He was unhappy with some incidents at the conclave, which I shall come to later, and was determined to issue a reforming constitution.

His two immediate successors, Popes Benedict XV and Pius XI, saw no need to amend Pius X's constitution. However, three popes since then have each issued a new constitution, building on that of Pius X but introducing new norms to take account of contemporary circumstances. The current regulations were promulgated in the Apostolic Constitution issued by Pope John Paul II on 23 February 1996, *Universi Dominici Gregis* ('The Shepherd of the Lord's Whole Flock'). It does not depart in substance from the constitution issued by Pope Paul VI in October 1975, *Romano Pontifici Eligendo* ('The Election of the Roman Pontiff'), but updates it in the light of present-day requirements, particularly in regard to the electoral process itself.

The procedures to be followed when the Pope dies or resigns are defined in precise detail by the Constitution. These procedures are initiated immediately. The Camerlengo is the key figure in the Church during a vacancy in the papacy. His role is not to be confused with that of the Dean of the College of Cardinals. The Dean is usually a senior cardinal who is elected to the office by the College. He presides at all its formal meetings, including those during the interregnum. If, however, he is over 80 years of age the duty falls on the sub-dean or the senior cardinal-elector. The Camerlengo, also a senior cardinal, is, however, appointed by the Pope. His principal function is to direct the organisation of the conclave and to preside over it. The office of Camerlengo dates from a reform of Pope Gregory VI (1073-85). He appointed a cardinal to supervise and administer the *Camera Apostolica,* the temporal possessions of the Holy See, including the Papal States. The holder of this office became known as the *Camerarius* (chamberlain) or, in popular language, the Camerlengo. In the Middle Ages the Camerlengo was one of the most important officials in the Holy See. In the era of the Papal States, he was effectively Minister of Finance, Public Works and Commerce. However, by the eighteenth century the office had become so powerful through the extent of its brief that Pope Pius VII (1800-23) decided to curtail the range of its activities to their present level in a radical reorganisation of papal government.

The Camerlengo's responsibilities during an interregnum begin as soon as the Pope dies. The Prefect of the Papal Household, a bishop, informs him of the death. The Camerlengo must verify the death in the presence of members of the Apostolic Camera, which administers the property of the Holy See, and of the Papal Master of Ceremonies. Traditionally death is verified by calling out the Pope's name three times and receiving no response.

The Camerlengo then authorises the official death certificate and informs the Vicar General of Rome, who in turn notifies the people of Rome officially that their bishop has died. The Dean of the College of Cardinals informs the cardinals, the diplomatic corps and governments. The Camerlengo formally seals the papal apartments, in which nobody is permitted to live during a vacancy. He takes possession of the Vatican Palace, the Lateran Palace and the Pope's summer home at Castel Gandolfo, in the Alban Hills, south-east of Rome.

Should the Pope die when outside Rome the College of Cardinals is to make the necessary arrangements to have the body transferred to the Vatican. If the burial is to take place in the Vatican Basilica, the Notary of the Chapter of St Peter's draws up the relevant document. Later, delegates of the Camerlengo and the Prefect of the Papal Household draw up documents certifying that the burial has taken place.

Photographs of a dying pope are not permitted, nor may his words be recorded on tape. Any requests to take photographs after his death for documentary purposes are directed to the Camerlengo, but he may only grant permission if the late pope is attired in his pontifical vestments.

If the late Pope has made a will concerning his property, letters and private documents his nominated personal executor is to carry out his wishes and report on the matter directly to the new Pope.

A pope may, of course, resign, though none has done so since Celestine V in the thirteenth century. His pontificate was brief and disastrous. A celebrated hermit, he was nearly 80 when elected to break a deadlock at one of the longest conclaves in history, lasting two years and two months. He found it impossible to cope with the responsibilities he had unwillingly assumed. The principal act of his reign was a decree declaring the pope's right to resign. He took advantage of it on 13 December 1294, only five months after his election, retiring to his hermitage. He might have done so in great fear and trepidation had he known that Dante's *Inferno,* written a few years later, was to consign him to Hell for making 'the great refusal' through cowardice. Medieval terrors of this kind would hardly trouble the minds of modern popes. The principal reason they have never contemplated resignation is the fear of creating a precedent. It would put pressure on successors to relinquish the papacy also, and perhaps for reasons other than those connected with their health or their age.

According to the Code of Canon Law, for the Pope's resignation to be valid it must be "freely and properly manifested but it is not necessary for it to be accepted by anyone" (can. 322.2). The key word is "freely" because a pope cannot be compelled to resign. However, there is no provision in canon law for a pope who falls so seriously ill that he is unable to function, for example, if he were to suffer from Alzheimer's Disease. In such circumstances there could be a serious crisis. It would be possible for the Pope to delegate in advance some of the powers normally reserved to himself to another person, perhaps a senior Vatican cardinal. But he cannot delegate the supreme authority; that belongs to the Pope alone. There is no deputy-Pope in the Catholic Church.

During a vacancy in the papacy the central

government of the Church is entrusted to the College of Cardinals solely for the conduct of ordinary business which cannot be postponed and for the preparation of all necessary arrangements for the conclave. The powers of the College are, therefore, extremely limited during an interregnum. It cannot assume the authority of the Pope or his power of jurisdiction in matters that pertain to him. Such matters must be reserved "completely and exclusively" to the future Pope. It has no power to modify any laws of the Church or to dispense from any part of them. The College may not alter in any way the Constitution for a papal election but must act strictly within the limits of its provisions. However, should a matter arise which in the view of the majority of cardinals cannot be postponed, the College may act in line with the majority opinion of the cardinals. The College may not dispose of any rights of the Holy See or allow them to lapse. All the cardinals are obliged to defend these rights.

3

The Decision Makers

The Pope is elected at what is called a conclave of the College of Cardinals held behind closed doors in the Sistine Chapel. The reason membership of the electoral college has been confined to the senior clergy of the Church in Rome since 1059 is because the Pope of the time, Nicholas II, saw it as a means of diminishing imperial manipulation of papal elections. The thinking was that, being confined to the senior clergy, whose position was not dependent on imperial favour, the electoral college would be less open to secular influence. These senior clergy became known as cardinals – from the Latin *cardo*, meaning a hinge or support – because they were the people on whom the administration of the Church in Rome, the *Curia Romana,* was said to 'turn'.

Until Nicholas II's reform papal elections varied in form. In the very early Church the incumbent would nominate his successor. Not surprisingly, this method of choosing a pope encountered much opposition. The Church in Rome then adopted a system developed in other churches where the clergy and people elected their local bishop. It was a democratic method well suited to a community, like Rome, that was then relatively small and homogenous. But when the interests of the Bishop of Rome extended beyond the city serious divisions arose about the election of the pope. Armed factions entered the fray and the pope had to seek the protection of the Roman civil power. As the Papal States developed the popes themselves grew wealthy and powerful and their office was much coveted. Emperors began to claim the right to approve the choice of pope and papal succession was sometimes delayed for lengthy periods awaiting the imperial sanction without which popes the papacy could be condemned to paralysis. Some progress towards freeing the Church from the imperial stranglehold was achieved by the eighth century when the papal electors were confined to the clergy of Rome. But the relief was temporary. Interference from influential families and corrupt civil officials became endemic and they resorted to bribery and violence in their efforts to control papal elections. The situation became so serious that radical steps had to be taken. A powerful advocate of reform appeared in the middle of the eleventh century, Hildebrand, a monk from Tuscany, who lived under no fewer than 14 popes and served six of them directly. Hildebrand exercised great influence on the election of five popes and helped frame the decree that, under Pope Nicholas II, confined the election of the Pope to cardinals. When Hildebrand was himself elected Pope in 1073 as Gregory VII he simply informed the German emperor of his election and did not seek or await imperial assent. His 12-year pontificate was marked by a growing liberty of the Church from secular influence and by a regeneration of its spiritual vigour.

In 1159 Rolando Bandinelli, a celebrated educationist in Bologna, was elected Pope at an assembly of 32 cardinals behind the high altar of St Peter's basilica. He received the votes of all but two, although it seems a third 'opponent' left before the end of the election because he would not miss his dinner.[5] However, Cardinal Octavian, the ambitious candidate of the Emperor, refused to accept the election on the spurious grounds that there had been a prior agreement among the cardinals that the election should not end until a candidate had been chosen unanimously.[6] Octavian set himself up as anti-Pope and a schism lasting for most of Alexander's 22-year reign ensued. When it ended in 1178 Alexander summoned the third Lateran Council the following year. He signed a decree based on a resolution of the Council that the candidate who got two-thirds of the votes should be recognised as Pope "by the universal church." The custom then regulating elections to other bishoprics was that a simple majority sufficed and any dispute could be settled on appeal to a superior. But, as the Council's second canon stated, "a special rule is made for the Roman Church because recourse cannot be had to a superior."[7]

The decrees of Nicholas II and Alexander III were of crucial significance. As Pope Paul VI remarked, any further dispositions have "merely applied and adapted this fundamental ordering of the election of the Roman Pontiff."[8] These two decrees were born out of particular crises. The third pillar of the papal election system, the conclave, was conceived as a drastic response to the indolence of the cardinals.

The longest vacancy in papal history followed the death of Clement IV in November 1268. It took the cardinals almost three years to elect his successor, Gregory X. He was neither a cardinal nor a priest and had to be summoned back from a pilgrimage to the Holy Land after his election in September 1271. This prolonged the papal succession by a further five months. Pope Gregory himself was determined to ensure such a scandalous delay would never recur. He resolved that cardinals at a papal election were to be kept in strict seclusion in one room, where they would eat, sleep and vote. The first enclosure of cardinals was actually in 1241 when they were forcibly herded into a room (three died from injuries received and the new pope excommunicated their assailant). But it was Gregory who made the enclosure mandatory. Thus a new word entered the language, 'conclave', derived from the Latin *cum clave* ('with a key'), referring to the locked place where the election takes place. Gregory's act compelled the cardinals to devote themselves exclusively to the election, free from distractions and outside pressures, and so speed up the process of papal succession. Gregory even laid down his own dietary regime for conclaves. He ordered that cardinals' food to be progressively reduced the longer a conclave continued. After three days they were to get only one dish at their noon and evening meals. After five days it was down to bread, wine and water. It worked! The next election, in 1276, lasted just over a day, the following one, seven days. Further changes in the election process were introduced by Pius IV in 1562 and the procedures he established have remained broadly the same ever since. The next conclave, to elect the 265th Pope, will be the 82nd since the system was first introduced. In the past the conclave was often held in the place where the previous pope had died. However, when Pope Sixtus V built the Quirinial Palace (now the seat of the Italian Government) in 1570 the conclave was sometimes held there until in 1878 when it was moved permanently to the Sistine Chapel.

The title 'Cardinal' was originally applied to any priest permanently attached to a church and was not necessarily confined to Rome. For example, it still survives in the two cardinals among the minor canons of St Paul's Cathedral, London, one of the most important churches of the Anglican Communion. Cardinals have traditionally been grouped into three orders, cardinal-bishops, cardinal-priests and cardinal-deacons. These designations do not imply degrees of ministerial ordination, since today all cardinals are bishops, but rather reflect their original purpose. The three orders of cardinals originated at different times. Cardinal-priests were originally the parish priests of Roman churches and today are normally archbishops of dioceses around the world. The symbolism of cardinals as clergy of the Church in Rome is still retained by assigning to members of the college special or titular churches in the Rome area. Cardinal-deacons cared for the poor in the seven districts of Rome and today are normally in full-time service with the Roman Curia. Cardinal-Bishops were created in the eighth century. They were the bishops of six dioceses in suburban Rome who at a time of great increase in papal business were drafted in to serve as the Pope's representatives. By the end of the first millennium the cardinals had become a papal court and the Pope's supreme advisory body and by the twelfth century the College was constituted in its present form. The six cardinal-bishops of the Latin rite are now normally the heads or former heads of the major departments of the Roman Curia. Eastern-rite patriarchs who receive the 'Red Hat' are also given the rank of Cardinal-bishop, but they are not assigned titles because their patriarchal inheritance preceded the emergence of cardinals in the Church. The original significance attached to membership of the three orders of cardinal gradually disappeared. Today there are about 18 cardinal-deacons, but the vast majority in the College are diocesan bishops and are therefore ranked as cardinal-priests. When attached to the Curia, cardinals are normally the Pope's special counsellors. Those living outside Rome also advise the Pope through general meetings and through membership of the various Vatican congregations. Occasionally, popes have honoured particular priests for important contributions, notably in theology, by creating them cardinals. These have included, for example, John Henry Newman, Yves Congar, Henri de Lubac, Hans Urs von Balthasar and Avery Dulles.

The most important collective function of the

cardinals is to elect the pope. In his Constitution Pope John Paul II acknowledges that theologically and canonically the conclave is not necessary for the valid election of the Pope. However, he says that a careful historical examination of the conclave "confirms the appropriateness of the institution, given the circumstances in which it originated and gradually took definitive shape, and its continued usefulness for the orderly, expeditious and proper functioning of the election itself, especially in times of tension and upheaval." He reaffirms the "millennial practice" of papal election by the cardinals only. The "universality of the Church is sufficiently expressed by the College of 120 electors, made up of cardinals coming from all parts of the world and from very different cultures." In the college is found "in a remarkable synthesis" the two aspects which characterise the figure and office of the Pope: *Roman*, because cardinals are symbolically linked to Rome through their titular churches in the city and its suburbs; *Pontiff of the Universal Church*, because the Pope is called visibly to represent Christ, who leads all the faithful to the pastures of eternal life."

Pope Paul VI, in his 1975 Constitution, gave a further reason: The increase in the number of cardinals has made the electoral college large but not unmanageably so. He considered enlarging the college by including non-cardinal members of the Synod of Bishops but in the end decided to reaffirm the principle of election by cardinals only. He concluded that, "as critical moments in the history of the Church and the papacy history has shown", it was undeniable that the electoral college should be named beforehand and should not be too numerous, so that it can be convened easily and without delay. He asserted that because the electoral college was appointed on a permanent basis it was less likely to be subject to influences and vested interests. He also believed it was constituted in such a way as to be able to act effectively when the Apostolic See is vacant.

Cardinals are not 'super bishops'. Before 1962 they were not required to be bishops, and before 1918, not even priests. Two of the most powerful cardinals of the nineteenth century, Ercole Consalvi (Secretary of State to Pope Pius VII) and Giacomo Antonelli (Secretary of State to Pope Pius IX) were never ordained priests. Both were deacons, but that did not diminish their influence. Such was Antonelli's power that he was able to keep Cardinal Pecci, Archbishop of Perugia and the future Pope Leo XIII, out of Rome because his ideas did not find favour within the Secretariat. The origin of the bishop's ministry goes back to apostolic times. Cardinals did not emerge until the sixth century as part of developments in Church government and administration.

The number of cardinals has varied throughout history. In the fourteenth century there were only between 18 and 26 and the cardinals of that time were happy to keep it that way; the fewer their number the greater their influence with the Pope. So important did the role of cardinal become in the Middle Ages that Roman and Italian families and European rulers went to great lengths to have relatives and friends appointed. Popes sometimes had great difficulty asserting the independence of the College. The prize sought by rulers was influence over the election of the Pope and, ultimately, control of Italy and Rome.

A decree of the reforming Pope, Sixtus V, in 1587 fixed the maximum number of cardinals at 70. This limit was not to be extended until 1959 when Pope John XXIII removed the ceiling altogether. Pope Paul, in a decree issued on 21 November 1970, fixed the maximum number of cardinal-electors at 120 but, in a radical move, excluded cardinals over 80 years of age from participating in the election. He formally reaffirmed this decision in his papal election constitution in 1975.[9] This ruling caused a minor sensation at the time because it was generally believed that a pope would never remove from any cardinal, regardless of age, his most ancient and most important right and privilege. However, it was with the intention of allowing the title to declare the message that Pope Paul named the decree *Ingravescentum Aetatem* ('The Increasing Burden of Old Age'). There were murmurs at the time of the first of the two papal elections in 1978 that the exclusion of the aged and venerable from the electoral college could call into question the validity of the election itself. But, nobody could gainsay the fact that a Pope has, as Paul VI asserted, "the prerogative, the right and the duty" to determine how the election is to be conducted. His constitution had stated clearly that none of the cardinals at the time of the conclave "must have passed their 80th birthday." However, at the first congregation of cardinals following Pope Paul's death, two octogenarians, Cardinals Ottaviani and Confalonieri, raised the issue for discussion, but the College had no authority to alter the constitution. Pope John Paul II retained this norm in his Constitution and went out of his way to justify it. "The reason for this provision is the desire not to add to the weight of such a venerable age the further burden of responsibility for choosing the one who will lead Christ's flock in ways adapted to the needs of the times." The effect of the age-barrier is that there is now no limit to the number of cardinals as long as the total under 80 years of age and, therefore, eligible to participate in a conclave, does not exceed 120. The Pope may, however, derogate from this norm. John Paul II did so twice, in 1998 and 2001, when he raised the number of cardinal-electors above the 120 his own Constitution permits.

One of the most significant features of the development of the College of Cardinals in recent decades is the extent to which it has been expanded and internationalised. From the inception of the College until recent years Italians dominated its membership, although the appointment of cardinals from outside Italy dates from the eleventh century. At the time of the election of Pope Gregory XVI in 1831, 54 of the 62 cardinals were Italians; at the election itself only 50 cardinals, all Italians, turned up. Italians were in the majority in the college because they held most senior curial posts, and a sizeable number of Italian dioceses traditionally had cardinal-archbishops. In addition, there was the hangover from the time of the Papal States when it was customary for the senior administrators to be cardinals. The 1903 conclave, which elected Pope Pius X, saw the presence of an American and an Irish cardinal at a papal election for the first time. By then the proportion of Italians had fallen although they were still in the great majority, 37 out of 62, or 60 per cent.

The proportions were precisely the reverse at the election of Pope John XXIII in 1958, when under a third of the cardinals were Italians. His predecessor, Pius XII, was the first Pope to alter radically the demographic make-up of the College by appointing a majority of non-Italians from all over the world in an effort to make it "a living symbol of the universality of the Church." However, because of the Second World War he held only two consistories, in 1946 and 1953. That meant that by 1958 the College had become rather geriatric and almost half the 51 cardinals who elected the 76-year-old Angelo Roncalli were older than the new Pope himself. John XXIII greatly expanded the College by abolishing the ceiling of 70 members and holding five consistories in four years, yet he actually made it more Italian than it had been when he became pope. It was his successors Paul VI and John Paul II who really internationalised the College.

The second conclave of 1978 was the largest in history – 112 cardinals, compared with 80 at the election of Paul VI. Sixty-two countries from all the continents are now represented. Africa, which got its first cardinal in 1960, has a dozen cardinal-electors. South America has 25. Italians have continued to be a minority, and a declining one.

Today they comprise around 17 per cent of the electoral college.

The expansion and internationalisation of the College reflects the enormous change in the demography of the Catholic Church over the past 100 years. The Catholic population was growing rapidly worldwide by the beginning of the twentieth century, but it was still overwhelmingly European in its leadership. Of the 983 dioceses in 1900 no fewer than 597, or almost 60 per cent, were in Europe. Brazil had a mere 17, the United States had 83, and in the whole continent of Africa there were only 17. About 700 bishops were at the opening of the First Vatican Council in December 1869, compared to 2500 at the opening of the Vatican Council II almost a century later. Of course, at the end of the nineteenth century many parts of the world were missionary territories governed by episcopal vicars and prefects apostolic with episcopal functions. They would progressively become dioceses during the twentieth century.

In Pope Leo XIII's time the Church was developing so rapidly that he established a total of 248 new dioceses, an average of almost ten in each year of his pontificate. He also encouraged and facilitated a considerable development in the missionary outreach of the Catholic Church, especially in Africa and Latin America, at a time when European colonial expansion was reaching its apogee. There has been a huge shift southwards in the population growth. In the short period 1910-1966, for example, the number of Catholics in South America grew from 47m to 137m, in Africa from

6m to 31m. Today the world's Catholic population has reached 1,000 million and 70 per cent live in the developing world. Emigration westward to the New World meant a rapid growth in the Catholic population in North America. One example: When James Gibbons was appointed the youngest bishop in the world in 1868 he administered the Church in the whole state of North Carolina where there were only 700 Catholics scattered over 50,000 square miles. Today one of the State's dioceses, Charlotte, alone has about 116,000 Catholics.

4

The Candidates

A conclave differs from most electoral assemblies in that there are no declared contestants. It is in the actual voting that the candidates emerge. While it is the exclusive right of cardinals to elect the Pope, their choice is not necessarily confined to one of their number. There is no job specification for the office of Pope. No qualifications are stipulated. In principle, any single adult male Catholic who has been baptised and confirmed may be elected pope. Two of the most powerful medieval popes, Innocent III and Gregory X, were not in priest's orders when they were elected. But, they were exceptions. Popes are habitually drawn from within the College of Cardinals. The last pope who was not was Urban VI in 1378. Most modern popes had been cardinals for several years but being new to the College is not necessarily a hindrance to election. Pope Benedict XV received the 'Red Hat' only three months before he became Pope in September 1914 and his successor, Pius XI, was a cardinal for only eight months. However, both came to the papacy with considerable experience. Usually, popes on election have been diocesan bishops or members of the Vatican Curia with extensive experience in pastoral work or in church government at central level. Over the centuries the assumption grew that only cardinals could become popes and this notion even found expression in the wording on ballot papers. At the 1903 conclave, for example, the inscription read: "I elect for Supreme Pontiff Most Rev. Lord *Cardinal...*" However, this false assumption has since been corrected and the ballot papers now carry the inscription "I elect as Supreme Pontiff..." and nothing else. Pope John Paul's Constitution has this advice for the cardinal-electors: "Having before their eyes God and the good of the Church they shall give their vote to the person, *even outside the College of Cardinals* (emphasis mine), who in their judgement is most suited to govern the universal church in a fruitful and beneficial way." If the choice is a layman, he is ordained priest and bishop, if a priest, he is ordained bishop. Women are excluded from the papacy because the Church has deemed that it has no authority to ordain them to the priesthood. This is essential: the Pope is Pope because he is Bishop of Rome.

Apart from obvious considerations like theological and administrative competence, the cardinals usually look for a person with rounded experience and of mature years. Taking 1700 as the benchmark year for the modern era, there have been 22 popes since then. Sixteen were elected in their sixties (12 in the age range 65-68), two in their seventies and four in their fifties. A known history of poor health would almost certainly disqualify a candidate in the cardinals' minds because they will not want the upheaval and expense of another conclave too soon. The young and athletic Pope John Paul II is said to have remarked wryly to a cardinal who queried the expense of building a swimming pool in the Vatican, that it was cheaper than holding another conclave. As it turned out, only two of the 264 popes have served longer than John Paul II, Pius IX and Leo XIII. Pontificates since 1700 have lasted an average of just over 13.5 years. Only six popes in that period died within five years or less. One of the greatest popes, Innocent III, would almost certainly find it impossible to be elected today because of his age and relative inexperience. He was not yet in priest's orders when elected in 1198, aged only 38. However, his 18-year pontificate (he died at 56) is regarded as the high point of the medieval papacy. He was a towering genius who imposed his personality and his authority on the Church and the world of his time by extending and enforcing the *plenitudo potestas* ('the plenitude of the power') of the See of Rome. He used this power to bring a centralised Christian society into being, to introduce radical reforms in clerical training, and to extend his authority as far north as Scandinavia and as far east as Cyprus and Armenia. He gave encouragement and support to the new orders of friars, the Dominicans and the Franciscans. He met St Francis of Assisi personally to approve the simple rule of life which he had drawn up for himself and his companions.

In choosing a pope the cardinal-electors have to

make judgement calls about the most important needs of the Church at the time. Would they want the papacy to continue on the course set by the late pope or is a change of direction desirable? Was the late pope preoccupied with particular concerns to the relative neglect of others? Was his pontificate too long or too short? What are the really critical questions he left behind? Is there among the candidates a pope who can help reinvigorate the faith commitment of a greatly increasing number of "detached" Catholics? With over two-thirds of the Catholic population now living in developing countries, is it now time for a Third World Pope? Is the Catholic Church sufficiently open to other Christians and to the wider world of believers and non-believers? In an age of mass images, what kind of figure would particular candidates cut on the world stage. The Holy Spirit uses fallible humans as his instruments of discernment. The choice of the cardinals can sometimes produce unexpected results. When they met in 1878 to choose a successor to Pius IX, the longest reigning pope in history (31 years), they clearly wanted a successor whose term would be short. So, they elected the frail-looking 68-year-old Archbishop of Perugia, Gioacchino Pecci, who became Leo XIII. Against all the odds Leo lived into his 94th year and his important and very eventful pontificate became the second longest in history, lasting over 25 years. It was said that his only malady was his age but since that was incurable it rendered him incapable of resisting others, and pneumonia finally overwhelmed him. Pope John Paul I was 65 and in apparent good health when elected in October 1978, but he died suddenly 34 days later. The cardinals who elected Angelo Roncalli in 1958 could hardly have imagined that the aged man they had chosen would have such a profound impact on the Church in a pontificate lasting less than five years.

The task facing any group of cardinal–electors is formidable. It is recorded that before the 1831 conclave Angelo Mai earnestly advised the cardinals to elect someone with the *faith* of St Peter, the *resolution* of the centurion Cornelius, the *good fortune* of Pope Silvester, the *elegance* of Pope Damasus, the *learning* of Pope Gelasius, the *piety* of Pope Gregory, the *strength* of Pope Eugenius, the *friendliness* of Pope Adrian, a *reconciler* of Churches like Pope Eugenius, a *wise counsellor* like Pope Julius, with the *generosity* of Pope Leo, *holy* like Pope Pius, with mental power like Pope Sixtus, *erudition* like Pope Benedict, *munificence* like Pope Pius VI, *courage and charity* like Pope Pius VII, *vigilance* like Pope Leo XII, and the *legislative skills* of Pope Pius VIII.[10] Cardinals are too experienced not to recognise that unreasonable expectations bring inevitable disappointment. No one human being can combine all the desired virtues. Of course, as a distinguished philologist and future cardinal, Angelo Mai was well aware of that, but he wanted to challenge the cardinals to set their sights high. Cardinal-electors will be conscious that, above all, their task is to choose a religious leader. Andrew Greeley has remarked that "if the head of a church is a superb administrator, a brilliant diplomat, a dazzling financier administrator, and a Solomon at conflict resolution, but is not effective in the religious dimension of his job, then he has failed as a leader."[11] Essentially, the cardinals will be seeking a pope who as far as possible incorporates in his person the gifts of both guardian and prophet; a guardian, to promote, protect and defend the integrity of the Church's teaching and mission in all its richness and fullness, and to proclaim it joyfully; a prophet with a vision to understand the broader picture, to illuminate the transcendent and address contemporary questions in a way that connects persuasively with the dominant culture of the time.

The lead-up to a papal election is always alive with speculation about its outcome, an "immense buzz of flies and wasps" as a commentator once remarked. However, it is wise to be sceptical of pundits who claim to predict the outcome of a papal election. There is an old Roman aphorism that the one who goes into a conclave as pope comes out a cardinal. It is only by chance that one can predict how 120 or so men from different backgrounds and cultures will vote in a secret ballot, especially when the Constitution specifically prohibits any pacts or promises. Of the last 15 popes only three – Leo XIII, Pius XII and Paul VI – could be said to have been favourites before their election. Two names which scarcely merited a mention in the acres of newsprint devoted to forecasting the outcomes of the two conclaves of 1978 were Albino Luciani and Karol Woytyla, who emerged as Popes John Paul I and John Paul II. If the cardinals surprised everybody in 1978 (twice) it is likely they will do so again next time.

As always following a long pontificate the vast majority of the cardinal-electors will be attending their first conclave. However, the notion that this means the next Pope will be cast in his predecessor's image is contradicted by historical experience. Owen Chadwick has written about the "law of elective constitutions" by which electors always look to fulfil a need not met under the previous regime.[12] A familiar experience in politics, it also applies to the Papacy. Pius XII was very different from John XXIII, as he was from Paul VI. Cardinals who have been very close to the late Pope usually have a greatly reduced chance of election. This is all the more so if a person has been in a powerful, highly visible position for some time. A good illustration of this is the tradition against electing secretaries of state.

After the Pope the Secretary of State is the most senior member of the Church's central government, with a role roughly equivalent to that of Prime Minister/Foreign Secretary rolled into one. It is a politically sensitive office and its holder inevitably acquires as many adversaries as friends. Over the past 330 years numerous secretaries of state have entered papal elections as favourites but only one, Pius XII in 1939, has come out as the Pope. Popes who seek to 'nominate' their successors rarely achieve their objective. Pope Pius IX, who ruled for 31 years, had appointed all the cardinals attending the conclave of 1878. He had made it known that he considered Cardinal Luigi Bilio, the principal author of the Syllabus of Errors and his closest collaborator, the best choice as his successor, but the Cardinals thought differently, and very decisively so by choosing Cardinal Pecci on the third ballot. The cardinal-electors usually exercise an independence of mind when they meet in conclave.

Modern cardinals have a number of distinct advantages over their predecessors. Today they are much more numerous and are scattered all over the world, yet they actually know each other better than was normally the case a hundred years ago. Those who live outside Rome visit the city very regularly for meetings of the Vatican bodies of which they are members or for meetings of the World Synod of Bishops or consistories of cardinals held periodically. Jet transport has facilitated the development of a whole new dimension in the understanding cardinals have of each other's strengths and weaknesses. When they gather in conclave they will not be meeting as strangers. It is fanciful to imagine them being manipulated by "Rome" in the choice of pope, even supposing Rome (meaning the Curia) to be all of one mind. The Curia itself is now much more international than in the past and a number of cardinals who hold senior positions within it are former diocesan bishops familiar with the realities of pastoral and parish life. In any case, most diocesan bishops, cardinals included, have a robust respect for their office and do not see themselves as branch managers of a multinational corporation. There is normally a healthy tension between the centralising impulses of Rome and the appropriate autonomy of the local church.

5

The Prologue

When the Camerlengo has formally confirmed the Pope's death the senior cardinals from each of the three orders of cardinal – bishop, priest and deacon – convoke a general congregation of the College. All cardinal-electors not legitimately impeded are obliged to attend each general congregation. Cardinals over 80 who are excluded from the papal election may attend the general congregations if they choose. If he is an elector the Dean of the College of Cardinals is to preside at meetings of the general congregations. If he is not, the sub-Dean is to preside and if he, too, is excluded by age, the senior cardinal-elector is to do so.

At the first general congregation the presiding cardinal is to read the part of the Constitution pertaining to the vacancy of the Apostolic See and cardinals are to be given time to raise questions about the meaning and the implementation of the norms.

The Constitution emphasises at several points the importance of a faithful adherence to the norms and to the obligation of the cardinals to maintain secrecy. At the first general congregation they are to take the following oath:

> *We, the Cardinals of the Holy Roman Church, of the Order of Bishops, Priests and Deacons, promise, pledge and swear, as a body and individually, to observe exactly and faithfully all the norms contained in the Apostolic Constitution* Universi Dominici Gregis *of the Supreme Pontiff John Paul ll, and to maintain rigorous secrecy with regard to all matters in any way related to the election of the Supreme Pontiff or those which, of their very nature, during the vacancy of the Apostolic See, call for the same secrecy.*

Each cardinal is then required to add that he personally does so promise, pledge and swear. With his hand on the Gospels, he says: "So help me God and the Holy Gospels which I touch with my hand."

The admonition about secrecy is phrased in very strong terms and the Constitution repeats it more than once. The oath above speaks of "rigorous secrecy". However, it is not clear why the oath should cover general congregations since, as the Constitution states, these meetings are "solely for the conduct of ordinary business and of matters which cannot be postponed and for the preparation of everything necessary for the election of a new pope." Most of the matters decided at meetings of the general congregations will become public anyway. Pope John Paul may have had in mind unforeseen matters of a sensitive nature. For example, at the conclaves of 1878 and 1903, when Italian troops occupied Rome and fears were raised for the security and freedom of the electors, delicate negotiations were carried out between senior cardinals and the Italian Government to ensure that there would be no interference with the election. Nevertheless, the emphasis on secrecy in Pope John Paul's constitution is more insistent than in those of his predecessors. This may have something to do with his experience of the first conclave of 1978, from which there were several leaks, and the Camerlengo of the time, Cardinal Jean Villot, had to warn the cardinals before the second conclave about the obligation of secrecy.

Important decisions during the interregnum are the responsibility of daily general congregations of the cardinals. Routine matters are dealt with by a smaller group, called a Particular Congregation, made up of the Camerlengo and three cardinals-assistants chosen by lot from each of the three orders. The cardinal-assistants serve for three days and are then replaced by three others similarly elected.

The Constitution stipulates that at one of the general congregations immediately following the first one, the cardinals, on the basis of a prearranged agenda, are to deal with the more urgent matters concerning the election. The Constitution specifies the following matters for decision:

- To set the dates and make the necessary arrange-ments for the funeral rites of the deceased Pope, to be celebrated on nine consecutive days. Except for special reasons burial is to take place between the fourth and sixth day after death;

- To arrange for the destruction of the symbols of the papal office, the Fisherman's Ring and the lead seal with which Apostolic letters are dispatched;

- To see that a commission, comprising the Camerlengo and cardinals who formerly held the office of Secretary of State and Prefect of the Pontifical Commission for Vatican City State, ensures that rooms are made ready for lodging the cardinals during the conclave. The next conclave will be the first in which the Domus Sanctae Marthae ('St Martha's House'), a new accommodation block within the grounds of the Vatican, will be used to accommodate the cardinal-electors. At previous conclaves temporary cells were erected for the cardinals in the area around the Sistine Chapel; this accommodation was spartan and uncomfortable;

- To assign rooms by lot to the cardinal-electors;

- To see that the Sistine Chapel is prepared so that the election process can be carried out in a smooth and orderly manner and with the maximum discretion;

- To entrust to two ecclesiastics, "known for their sound doctrine, wisdom and moral authority", the task of presenting to the cardinals two well-prepared meditations and to fix the day when the first is to be given. The meditations should focus on the grave duty falling on the cardinals and the need to act with the right intention for the good of the universal church;

- To approve, on the proposal of the Administration of the Apostolic See, a budget of expenses occurred during the period from the death of the pope until the election of his successor;

- To read any documents left by the pope for the College of Cardinals;

- To fix the day and the hour of the beginning of the voting process.

In the past, the last of these decisions was the most controversial. The time allowed between the death of a pope and the beginning of the conclave has varied throughout history. In the twelfth century it was only three days. But, by the eighteenth century this had changed. It was reported in 1823 that time was required "for electors to assemble from distant provinces and even from foreign countries" and so the conclave of that year was delayed for 33 days.[13] Later that century fears emerged that a long interregnum could leave a dangerous vacuum and the waiting time was cut to ten days. This was convenient for Italians but not for cardinals from other parts of the world, though even for Italians it could sometimes prove difficult. It is recorded that in 1846 Pope Pius IX was elected by a conclave "that was inspired so swiftly by the Holy Spirit that the Cardinal-Archbishop of Milan arrived too late."[14] Until the mid-twentieth century the slow pace of transport made it particularly difficult for cardinals from outside Italy to reach Rome in time. John

McCloskey of New York and Paul Cullen of Dublin set out to attend the conclave of February 1878 but the new Pope (Leo XIII) was elected before they reached Rome. Both would have been attending their first and only conclave. Cardinal James Gibbons of Baltimore, the first American to attend a papal election, only made it to Rome in time for the 1903 conclave because the Cardinal-Secretary of State had alerted him to Pope Leo's declining health three weeks before he died. Cardinal Patrick Moran of Sydney was not so lucky; the journey from Australia took ten weeks. In 1914 the Americans made a major issue of the timing of the conclave. Two of their cardinals, Gibbons and William O'Connell of Boston arrived in Naples with little time to spare. O'Connell left Gibbons and hired a car. However, it broke down and neither cardinal arrived in time. O'Connell made a furious protest. This did not have any effect until eight years and another papal election later when a decree by the newly-elected Pius XI on 1 March 1922 stipulated that the conclave must not start before the fifteenth day after the Pope's death but must not be delayed beyond the eighteenth day. With the later addition of a further two days (to the twentieth) this norm has been retained ever since, even though air travel means that cardinals can reach Rome within a few days wherever they may be. A practical benefit is that it affords the cardinals time to talk informally and to take soundings, to lobby and be lobbied, and to refine their judgements in the focused context of an imminent election. Of the two conclaves in 1978 the first began on the twentieth day, due principally to the fact that August is the traditional holiday month in Rome. The second, however, began fifteen days after the sudden death of Pope John Paul I in late September. The conclaves of 1958 and 1963 each began on the sixteenth day.

All cardinal-electors are obliged to attend the conclave unless prevented by illness or by some other 'grave impediment' which must, however, be recognised as such by the general congregation. Cardinals who arrive after the conclave has begun but before a pope has been elected must be allowed to take part in the election at whatever stage it has reached. No cardinal-elector may be excluded from attending the conclave, even if he has been excommunicated or is under an interdict or any other impediment. For the purpose of the conclave only these censures are considered suspended.

The Domus Sanctae Marthae, where the cardinals will live during the conclave, as well as the Sistine Chapel and any other areas reserved for liturgical celebrations, will be closed to all unauthorised persons for the duration of the conclave. The general congregation must make provision to ensure that no one approaches the cardinal electors while they are in transit from Domus Sanctae Marthae to the Sistine Chapel or any other part of the Vatican.

The Constitution stipulates that the following assistants may enter the conclave area, though none is allowed in the Sistine Chapel when a ballot in being held:

• The secretary of the College of Cardinals, who is an archbishop;

- The Papal Master of Ceremonies;
- Assistants to take care of the sacristy;
- A number of priests from religious orders to hear confessions in the principal languages;
- A surgeon and a general physician, with one or two medical assistants;
- Other personnel approved by the general congregation to take care of the needs of the conclave.

The Secretary of the Conclave and the Papal Master of Ceremonies will swear an oath before the Camerlengo promising to observe inviolable secrecy about "each and every matter" concerning the election. They, in turn, acting on behalf of the Camerlengo, will administer the oath to all other non-cardinals permitted to enter the conclave area. Besides pledging secrecy regarding any information concerning the conclave that may come their way, the assistants specifically promise not to use any type of transmitting or receiving instrument, nor devices designed to take pictures. Presumably, what the Constitution wants to prevent here is the exploitation of the conclave by those in a privileged position who may be tempted to write about it afterwards.

6

The Pledges

Cardinal-electors will celebrate Mass for the election of the Pope in St Peter's Basilica on the morning of the first day of the conclave. In the afternoon they will assemble in the Pauline Chapel in the Vatican and will walk in procession to the Sistine Chapel to begin the election process. From the moment the conclave begins until the result is announced, the cardinal-electors are not allowed to communicate by writing, telephone or by any other means with persons outside the Vatican. An exception is made in cases of urgent necessity, with the prior approval of the Camerlengo and the three other members of the Particular Congregation. Cardinal-electors may not receive communication of any kind from outside. They are not allowed to listen to radio or watch television and no newspapers or periodicals are permitted.

At the beginning of the conclave the cardinals take a solemn oath giving a number of explicit undertakings. The Cardinal-Dean or the senior cardinal-elector reads out the text of the oath. The cardinal-elector must take the oath individually and collectively:

We, the Cardinal-electors present in this election of the supreme pontiff promise, pledge and swear, as individuals and as a group, to observe faithfully and scrupulously the prescriptions contained in the apostolic constitution of the supreme pontiff Pope John Paul II, Universi Dominici Gregis, *published on 22 February 1996. We likewise promise, pledge and swear that whichever of us by divine disposition is elected Roman Pontiff will commit himself to carry out* munus Petrinum *('the service of Peter') of pastor of the universal church and will not fail to affirm and defend strenuously the spiritual and temporal rights of the Holy See. In a particular way, we promise and swear to observe with the greatest fidelity and with all persons, clerical or lay, secrecy regarding everything that in any way relates to the election of the Roman pontiff and regarding what occurs in the place of the election, directly or indirectly related to the results of the voting; we promise and we swear not to break this secret in any way, either during or after the election of the new pontiff, unless explicit authorisation is granted by the same pontiff; and never to lend support or favour to interference, opposition or any other form of intervention, whereby secular authorities of whatever order and degree or any group of people or individuals might wish to intervene in the election of the Roman Pontiff.*

Each cardinal, in order of seniority, will then place his hand on the Gospels and say: "I do so promise, pledge and swear, so help me God and these Holy Gospels which I touch with my hand."

The Constitution binds all participants in the conclave to maintain confidentiality regarding the election for life. Cardinals are forbidden to reveal to anybody, directly or indirectly, information about the voting. The stress placed on secrecy within the conclave is essentially to protect the independence of judgement and the freedom of decision and action of the cardinal-electors. However, it is difficult to see how the publication of the voting results at the end of the conclave could possibly compromise the freedom of individual cardinal-electors or the secrecy of the ballot box. There is no apostolic tradition behind withholding ballot results from the public. It dates only from the 1904 constitution for a papal election. We know of the voting record of a number of conclaves since then thanks to the literary remains of participating cardinals. The papal electoral system has an extremely long and mostly honourable tradition of which the Catholic Church has a right to be proud. This is why the voting record is of genuine interest, especially to Catholics. It is a graph that can be of help in understanding the process of discernment that was undertaken in their name behind closed doors. The lack of accurate data does nothing to promote reliable analysis in today's media-driven age.

The Constitution prohibits the introduction into the conclave – or their use should they be intro-duced – of technical equipment for the recording, reproduction or transmission of voices or images. Two "trustworthy technicians" are to ensure that no audiovisual equipment for recording or transmitting has been installed in the Sistine Chapel or surrounding areas. Anyone responsible for infringing the secrecy of the conclave by means of such equipment "will be subject to grave penalties according to the judgement of the future pope". Regular sweeps are to be made in the conclave area to ensure it is free of bugging devices.

Veto forbidden

Cardinals and anyone taking part in the preparation or conduct of the conclave are bound under pain of automatic excommunication not to accept the task of proposing a veto on behalf of any body or person. Pope John Paul's Constitution is categorical about prohibiting external interference: "The intervention of any lay power of whatever grade or order is absolutely excluded", it declares. The Constitution's stricture is all embracing:

> Confirming the prescriptions of my predecessors I forbid each and every cardinal, present and future, as also the Secretary of the Conclave and all those persons taking part in the preparation and carrying out of everything necessary for the election, to accept under any pretext whatsoever, from any civil authority whatsoever, the task of proposing a veto or so-called *exclusiva*, even under the guise of a simple desire, or to reveal

such either to the entire body assembled together or to individual electors, in writing or by word of mouth, either directly and personally or indirectly and through others, both before the election begins or for its duration. I intend this prohibition to include all possible forms of interference, opposition and suggestion whereby secular authorities of whatever order and degree, or any individual or group, might attempt to exercise influence on the election of the Pope.

The background to the veto prohibition is fascinating. The concept of a secular veto was not confined to papal elections. At various times throughout history European rulers sought to control the appointment of bishops in their territories. State control of the episcopacy probably reached its peak under weak popes in the fourteenth century. In 1376 the King of Portugal forbade the pope to appoint any bishops without his consent. Thirty years earlier the German emperor Charles IV had received the pope's permission to exercise control over all episcopal nominations in the empire. Still earlier the Hungarian bishops had complained to the pope that no bishop had been promoted for 23 years except at the king's command.[15] In the nineteenth century the British government considered it important to try to secure a decisive say in the appointment of bishops in Ireland where the influence of the Catholic Church was considerable. In 1816 the Irish bishops protested vigorously to Rome when the Prefect of the Congregation of Propaganda Fide, Cardinal Litta, instructed them to accept a right of a qualified veto by the British government on episcopal appointments in return for Catholic emancipation. In face of the bishops' hostile reaction Rome prudently let the instruction lie. Archbishop Daniel Murray of Dublin told the Synod of Thurles in 1850 that had they not objected so strongly in 1816 many of the bishops present would never have been appointed.

Throughout much of its history the papacy was subject to pressure from civil rulers who sought to influence the election of the pope. From the sixteenth century the Catholic powers of France, Spain and Austria secured influence over the election by means of a veto – called the 'right of exclusion' (*jus exclusivae*). The influence of King Louis XIV of France prevented the election of Innocent XI in 1669, but he became Pope after the next vacancy in 1676. Austria vetoed two cardinals at the conclave in Venice in 1800 and Cardinal Chiaramonti (Pius VII) was elected as a compromise after a three months' stalemate. In 1823 the votes were divided between Cardinals Severoli, Castiglioni and della Genga. Austria vetoed the first to secure the election of the second but the conclave chose the third (Leo XII). Castiglioni (Pius VIII) was elected at the following conclave in 1829, but died 20 months later. Cardinal Giustiniani seemed certain of election in 1831 when the Spanish interposed with a veto. In 1846 the cardinal bearing the Austrian veto arrived too late.

The claim of the Powers to have a *right* to exclude particular cardinals from election was at best based on precedent, an assumed prerogative of custom, as it were. It was not a right in law because no such right had ever been promulgated. In fact, all papal declarations on the veto were negative. Pius IV in 1562 ordered cardinals to elect "without regard to the interference of secular rulers or to other human considerations". In 1732 a Bull issued by Clement XII repeated the words used by Pius IV. In the minutes of the commission of cardinals appointed to draw up this Bull the veto is explicitly characterised as an abuse. As one expert on the veto wrote, to debar precisely the most capable candidates is "an onerous limitation of the liberty of the electors and injurious to the Church."[16] In 1871 Pope Pius IX issued a Bull, *In Hac Sublimi*, forbidding any interference of secular powers in papal elections. Despite these papal pronouncements, however, the Church was in a weak position to resist the veto since it was itself deeply involved in politics through the Papal States and because the principle of the veto had been conceded in the appointment of bishops. Also, for those Powers that chose to exercise the veto it mattered who became pope – or, more precisely, who did not become pope, for their influence was essentially negative. Most of their citizens were Catholics and the influence of the Church and the papacy on their political fortunes could sometimes be profound. Because of the nature of the office, the papacy could not remain above politics, however much a particular pope might wish to, because his preaching, teaching and pastoral decisions could have political consequences. The German Chancellor, Bismarck, once remarked sardonically that the pope was "a man who disposes of the consciences of two hundred million people and is, therefore, a mighty monarch." The Catholic Powers had a vested interest in trying to ensure that a cardinal considered unsympathetic to their interests was not elected pope. A cardinal on behalf of the ruler formally declared the veto in the conclave if it appeared likely that a person judged to be unacceptable was likely to be chosen.

There were two tactical judgements the cardinal had to make. Firstly, to decide if a veto were truly necessary, for it would be both useless and foolish to use it if the pattern of the voting indicated that it could have no effect. If it were judged to be necessary he then had to decide at what point it would be most effective to exercise it. A good sense of timing was essential because the veto could be used only once. Since deviations in voting can be unpredictable from ballot to ballot, and a ruler might be unhappy with more than one cardinal, delay in using a formal veto would be well advised until a clear trend had emerged. The veto was essentially an option of last resort.

The veto was last exercised at the 1903 conclave, one of the most remarkable in the history of the modern papacy. It had drama, emotion, surprise, and intrigue. The cardinals began the election in the general expectation that they would have chosen a new pope within a couple of days. However, the election took twice as long. The Cardinal-Bishop of Crakow, Jan Puzyna, exercised the veto on behalf of Emperor Franz Josef of Austria. His target was Cardinal Mariano Rampolla del Tindaro, a Sicilian who held doctorates in four subjects and was fluent in five languages. He had been Secretary of State for the last 16 years of Pope Leo XIII's pontificate.

On doctrinal matters Rampolla was determinedly orthodox and was later to become head of the Holy Office, the Cardinal Ratzinger of his day. What concerned the Habsburg Emperor was Rampolla's influence on Leo XIII in determining papal foreign policy. The Pope and his Secretary shared a growing conviction that the world was changing in a way that was not propitious for the future of dynasties. Leo's endorsement of democracy as the best system of government in the encyclical *Immortale Dei* (1885) displeased the Emperor. The Pope's words were cautious and implied no ringing affirmation of democracy, but they did strike a new note in papal declarations on civil society. According to a diplomatic dispatch Vienna was convinced that Rampolla favoured republican democracy to the detriment of monarchies.[17] Austria was particularly unhappy with Leo's policy of *rapprochement* towards Republican France. From Rome's perspective the aim was to rescue the French Church from the catastrophe of isolation in the hostile environment of state-sanctioned anti-Catholicism. Leo and his Secretary were reading the signs of the times and these were telling them that there could be no return to the past in France. The fruits of their diplomacy were not to be fully harvested for several generations for *royalisme* continued to divide the French Church. However, the lasting effect of Leo's policy was to make it clear at the highest level that the Church was not tied to the *ancien regime*.[18] The Emperor also resented Rampolla's interest in the condition of the discontented southern Slavs who were subject to the Empire. While there is evidence from several sources that Rampolla could sometimes be difficult to deal with, he hardly merited the scathing criticism contained in a secret dispatch from the Austrian Ambassador to the Holy See in 1897: "Pious, hard on himself, suspicious, dissimulating and extremely violent in his sentiments, he represents all the faults of a natural Sicilian... No one other than the cardinal has used every occasion to show openly his aversion to us. With his hypocritical and violent character, he is always prepared to use his power in a manner contrary to our interests."[19]

Now that Leo was dead Franz Josef wished to see his foreign policy buried with him and that meant exercising the veto against Rampolla. Cardinal Puzyna, a member of an old Polish aristocratic family, was the second in a line of reforming bishops in Crakow, the traditional intellectual and spiritual centre of Poland. He had his own reasons for not wanting Rampolla and there is evidence to suggest that he himself instigated the veto.[20] Like many Poles, he would have considered that Pope Leo and his Secretary of State had been neglectful of the interests of Poland, which at that time was carved up between Austria, Prussia and Russia. Rampolla was the favourite going into the conclave. With 29 votes he had a lead of 13 after the second ballot and needed only 13 more to reach a two-thirds majority. Cardinal Gibbons was sitting to his right and the prospects appeared so favourable for the ex-Secretary of State that he turned and congratulated him.[21] Puzyna became alarmed. He requested the Camerlengo and the Conclave Secretary to read out the veto. The Camerlengo said he wouldn't and the Secretary that he couldn't. Puzyna was left with no option but to declare it himself. When he told Rampolla what he was about to do, he was advised to consult the tribunal of his conscience.[22] The veto brought an immediate and definitive response from the Camerlengo. He declared the communication to be unacceptable. It could have no official or unofficial status.[23]

However, by the time the veto was introduced the momentum for Rampolla had already expired. In a gesture of defiance against the veto, the conclave actually increased Rampolla's support by one in the ballot immediately following its declaration. But in reality his vote had already become frozen at just under 50 per cent, so the veto was not the determining factor in the election. Leo had raised the prestige of the papacy to an extraordinary height. That was why Rampolla, the collaborator devoted to Leo's grand designs drew such strong support.

In the end, however, the cardinals concluded that the new head of the Church should be a man of an essentially different type from his predecessor. After years of giving preference to the 'Ministry of Foreign Affairs' it was high time to think of the 'Ministry of the Interior.' They wanted a pope who had matured in the office of bishop and would be most interested in pastoral questions.[24] The Patriarch of Venice, Cardinal Giuseppi Sarto, had no connection with the Curia. He had come to the conclave with wide pastoral experience, as a parish priest, spiritual director and diocesan administrator. As Bishop of Mantua from 1884 he revitalised the diocese. Both there and in Venice, where he was Patriarch for ten years, he acquired a reputation for doctrinal rigour combined with acute pastoral instincts. Starting from a low base of just five votes he was the only candidate whose support increased in every round and he was elected on the seventh ballot with 50 of the 62 votes and became Pope Pius X. He was the compromise the cardinals opted for, and decisively so in the end, when it became clear that they were split down the middle on Rampolla's candidature. The French cardinal, Francois-Desire Mathieu, recalled how perplexed Puzyna was by the criticism he received when, after all, he had been the cause of the election of a good pope. "His Eminence flatters himself; he was not the cause of anything", was Mathieu's dismissive remark.[25] The conclave secretary, Archbishop Merry del Val, confirmed this some years later. He was in an excellent position to observe the mood of the conclave with some degree of detachment because he was not yet a cardinal and had no vote. "It is my certain conviction", he wrote of the veto, "that (Rampolla) would never have been elected in any case, for the majority of electors was firmly intent on choosing some other candidate."[26] The 'law of electoral constitutions' brought about a change of direction in 1903, and it was to do so again at the next conclave in 1914 when Cardinal Giacomo della Chiesa was elected. He was a protégé of Rampolla and became his close collaborator (serving under him in the Madrid Nunciature and in the Secretariat of State). Rampolla was not to see della Chiesa's elevation to the papacy as Benedict XV; he had died suddenly, aged 70, nine months before. Benedict revived the tradition of Leo's diplomacy but, in the terrible scourge of the First World War, had limited success.

Whatever about the actual effect of the veto – this "shocking anachronism", as Cardinal Mathieu called it[27] – the very fact that it had been exercised affected Pope Pius X deeply. He was to take speedy and decisive action. Only five months after his election he issued a short decree abolishing the veto absolutely.[28] The decree declared that the Holy See had never approved of the civil veto, though previous legislation had not succeeded in preventing it. The force of the new pope's injunction against the veto could not have been expressed more strongly. "In virtue of holy obedience, under threat of the divine judgement, and pain of excommunication *latae sententiae* (i.e. automatically)", he forbade the cardinals and all others who take part in the conclave, to receive the office of proposing a veto in "whatever manner", including intercessions, "by which the lay powers endeavour to intrude themselves on the election of the pontiff". He declared: "Let no man infringe this our inhibition… under pain of incurring the indignation of God Almighty and his Apostles, SS Peter and Paul."[29]

Pius X's successors, in updating the regulations, have reiterated his strictures against the veto. In a sense, history has come full circle. Under the current Constitution, promulgated by Puzyna's fellow-Pole and his successor as Cardinal-Archbishop of Crakow, Pope John Paul II, cardinals in conclave are obliged to swear a solemn oath "never to lend support or favour to interference, opposition or any

form of intervention, whereby secular authorities…
might wish to intervene in the election of the Roman
Pontiff."

An interesting sidelight on that conclave is that
the archives of the Irish archdiocese of Armagh
contain a record of the voting kept by Cardinal
Michael Logue. However, Logue does not appear
to have been well attuned to the politics of the
conclave, judging from a note he wrote to the
Archbishop of Dublin from Rome: "The factions
and the intrigues of which you read much in the
papers I could see little of, though I took my meals
with the Italian cardinals and was thrown very much
among them."[30]

No pacts or promises

Canvassing by cardinals on behalf of particular
choices is permitted and has always been a feature
of papal elections. But striking deals or bargains to
secure votes is not allowed. Pope John Paul's
Constitution advocates discussion of the election
among cardinals but, in the light of the experience
at some past conclaves, absolutely forbids any pact,
agreement or promise that would oblige them to
give or deny their vote to a particular person. Any
such commitment would be null and void and "no
one shall be bound to observe it." Any cardinal
violating this prohibition is automatically excommunicated. At the 1903 conclave the influential
German cardinal, Georg Kopp of Breslau, not
wishing the veto to be used, sought to achieve a

compromise with Rampolla in which, if he withdrew, he could assume the role of 'Grand Elector' able to nominate a candidate of his choice. Rampolla refused to withdraw or to discuss any candidate.[31]

The Constitution also forbids any pre-election arrangements by which cardinals commit themselves jointly to a certain course of action should one of them be elected. Any such promises, even if made under oath, would also be null and void. The Constitution urges cardinals not to be guided by friendship or aversion, by interference by persons in authority or by pressure groups, by suggestions in the media or by force, fear or the pursuit of popularity.

During the vacancy in the Papacy and especially during the conclave, Pope John Paul's Constitution urges Catholics to "persevere with one heart in prayer" that God may grant the Church a new pope "as a gift of his goodness and providence" and that "a speedy, harmonious and fruitful election may take place." In this way the election of the new pope "will not be something unconnected with the People of God and concerning the college of electors alone."

Simony

The current Constitution retains a censure on what Pope Paul VI called "the detestable crime of simony."[32] Pope John Paul's Constitution states: "If – God forbid – in the election of the Roman Pontiff the crime of simony were to be perpetrated, I decree and declare that all those guilty thereof shall incur automatic excommunication."

Simony was a major problem in the early Church and it persisted well into the Middle Ages. The Council of Chalcedon (451) forbade ordination for money and St Gregory the Great had to condemn simony forcefully in the following century. Trafficking in clerical appointments became widespread in the Middle Ages. Pope Alexander II (1061-73) deposed the Archbishop of Milan for simony. The Third Lateran Council (1179) outlawed it in any form, and also banned the holding of several benefices by one person or the promising of one before it was vacant. Despite all this, simony proved difficult to stamp out. It even invaded the medieval papacy. The anti-pope John XXIII (1410-15) was deposed because his election had been bought. But, when he agreed to resign and to recognise Pope Martin V (1417-31) he was made Cardinal-Bishop of Tusculum. The name 'John', until then the most popular for popes, was not to be chosen again until Cardinal Angelo Roncalli was elected Pope in 1958. He took the same title, John XXIII, as the medieval anti-pope.

Pope Alexander VI (1431-1503) secured the papacy largely through bribery. This caused his successor, Julius II (1443-1513), to issue a definitive prohibition against simony in papal elections. His decree, *De Fratrum Nostrorum* (1503) declared null and void every pontifical election brought about by simony. This remained in force until 1904 when Pope Pius X declared that an act of simony does not nullify the election of the pope and that the validity of the election may not be challenged for this reason. Every constitution issued since then adopted the same provision.[33] This was not in order to make it easier for anyone to buy his way into papacy or to exonerate anyone who may have done so. Indeed, simony is regarded so seriously that the Constitution takes the rare step of imposing automatic excommunication on those who attempt to break the law. The reason is to avoid the situation that would inevitably arise if there were any doubt about a man's election as pope. If this were invalid, the fact would probably not be discovered for some time – for years maybe, or even until he was already dead – and all appointments, the legislation and other important acts done by him as Pope would be invalid. The terrible uncertainty arising from this could be catastrophic for the Church and it is to avoid this evil that modern popes have removed the nullity of simoniacal election. The Church's law establishing the invalidity of offices provided out of simony has a very good reason behind it, but it is purely ecclesiastical law; it is man made. For a good reason – and there is good reason in this case – it can be exempted from. A legal act can be unlawful but still valid. A man who becomes Pope through simony acts unlawfully but he is still Pope. The likelihood of simony in a modern papal election is extremely remote. Quite clearly it would be a terrible thing if this were to happen. The scandal and the damage would be immense. But at least the evils mentioned above would be avoided.

In the Church of England ordinands or recipients of benefices were obliged to swear an oath under the Canons of 1604 that their offices were not secured through simony, but the practice persisted through the system of ecclesiastical patronage. It was not until the English Benefices Act of 1898 that more effective action was taken to try to eliminate simony.

7

The Voting

After the cardinals have taken the oath the Papal Master of Ceremonies gives the order *Extra Omnes* (literally, 'all out') to those not part of the conclave. Apart from the cardinals the only persons remaining in the Sistine Chapel are the Master of Ceremonies and the cleric who is to give the reflection. After this has been delivered they, too, must leave. The senior cardinal-elector then asks the cardinals if they are ready to begin or are there still doubts about the norms and procedures that require clarification. They may only be clarified, not altered. The cardinals are not permitted to cancel or modify in any way the norms and procedures laid down in the Constitution, even if they were to agree that this should be done.

The Constitution decrees that for the election of a pope to be valid one person must receive two-thirds of the votes if the numbers present are exactly divisible by three; if not, a two-thirds majority plus one. The reason for the extra vote in excess of two-thirds – which was first made mandatory by Pope Pius XII in his Constitution issued in 1945[34] – is to prevent any cardinal being decisive in his own election. If the cardinals have reached a stalemate after a prolonged period they have the option of resorting to one of two alternative methods of election:

- By an absolute majority, that is, 51 per cent of the votes.

- By a "run-off" between the two candidates who had the greatest number of votes in the last ballot.

These two alternative methods were among four approved in the 1975 constitution of Pope Paul VI. Conclaves can be greatly prolonged because one candidate is unable to secure two-thirds of the votes. If a minority within the conclave is sufficiently large and cohesive it can prevent the election of the majority's preferred choice. While it takes two-thirds of the votes to elect a candidate, only a third, plus one, is required to block his election. In these circumstances it is customary for a conclave to settle on a candidate acceptable to the majority and to at least as many of the minority as are necessary to make up two-thirds of the votes. A good example was the 1922 conclave, at which there were 53 cardinals, with 36 votes being required for election. The ex-Secretary of State, Cardinal Gasparri, reached 24 votes in the eighth ballot and Cardinal Lafontaine of Venice 23 votes in the eleventh, but neither could achieve the two-thirds majority. A compromise was found in the scholarly Archbishop of Milan, Cardinal Achille Ratti, whose five votes in the eighth ballot grew to 42, and election, in the fourteenth.

A conclave is essentially about discerning the collective mind of the cardinal-electors. It is a natural feature of any election process that voters support the candidate whose opinions are closest to their own. Typically, the first ballot votes are scattered over a large number of candidates. But, by the third ballot the votes begin to be concentrated on about four or five. 'Parties' have emerged. Roughly speaking, there are usually three 'parties' at papal elections, those who are happy with the *status quo* and wish its continuance, those who want change, and those of no resolute views either way. The third 'party' is the focus of the most vigorous canvassing by cardinals from the other two. The early front-runners often fade as alliances shift in response to changes in voting patterns. A candidate who barely figured to a significant extent in the early voting often begins to surface as the conclave moves towards its decisive phase. The two-thirds majority system is a discriminating means in deciding the election because it respects both majority and minority views. If a group within the conclave can command such a high proportion of the votes it ceases to be a 'party' and becomes a conclusive coalition. For this reason Pope Paul VI and John Paul II were anxious to ensure that it could not be easily discarded while also providing the cardinals with alternatives should it prove impossible for any candidate to get two-thirds of the votes. The changes made by Paul VI and John Paul II create the possibility of a pope being elected by an absolute majority – 51 per cent of the votes – for the first time. However, for this to happen there would have to be an extremely prolonged stalemate, such as has not occurred in any conclave for over 170 years. Pope Paul stipulated that the cardinal-electors could resort to an alternative if no one is elected after 22 ballots, but that they had to agree unanimously to adopt this course. Pope John Paul increased to 30 the number of ballots required before an alternative can be considered, but he also decreed that an absolute majority rather than unanimity is sufficient for an alternative to be adopted. It is notable that the only methods of electing the pope that are now valid all involve a majority vote of some kind. According to Pope John Paul such methods give "the greatest guarantee of clarity, straightforwardness, simplicity, openness and, above all, an effective and fruitful participation on the part of the cardinals."

Several methods of election approved in the past can no longer be used. One was by acclamation or by inspiration, when all the cardinals agree freely and spontaneously to one name. The most recent examples were in the seventeenth century when Clement X (1670-76) and his successor Innocent XI (1676-89) were chosen by acclamation. In the case of Clement (Cardinal Altieri) the crowd outside the conclave chanted 'Altieri Papa' and the cardinals within unanimously confirmed him. Election by acclamation was retained by Pope Paul VI but abolished by Pope John Paul II because he considered it no longer an apt means of interpreting the thought of an electoral college so great in number and so diverse in origin. Another alternative in Paul

VI's Constitution was election by delegation, in which the cardinals could agree to nominate a minimum of nine and a maximum of 15 cardinals to elect the pope. Pope John Paul also abolished this because it limits the responsibility of individual electors who would not be required to express their choice personally.

In the sixteenth century an intricate procedure was introduced to speed up the election, the *accesso*, a variation of the single transferable vote system used in some countries for political elections. After an indecisive ballot the cardinals were given the opportunity of transferring their votes to another candidate, that is, to 'accede' to his election. If the votes in the original ballot, added to those in the *accesso*, gave a candidate the required majority he was declared elected. The *accesso* was usually thought to favour the leader in the original ballot because he had acquired a momentum of votes and this tended to exercise an influence on the undecided. The *accesso* was complicated because the secrecy of the ballot could not be infringed, yet the ballot papers required exhaustive checking to ensure that no cardinal had voted for the same person twice. At the 1903 conclave the Camerlengo (Cardinal Oreglia) made the controversial decision not to allow it, on the grounds it was complicated and tended to yield surprises. This was an arbitrary decision. As one participant cardinal put it: "That the *accesso* is complicated cannot be denied. But why declare impracticable a method that has been used without interruption for many centuries?"[35] Pope Pius X's Constitution of 1904 abolished the *accesso*, but he also established a very important principle: that it is the cardinal-electors as a body – never the Camerlengo alone – who have the authority and responsibility of making any necessary decisions about voting procedures.[36] A biography of Cardinal Rampolla commemorating the tenth anniversary of his death was published in 1923 by the Vatican's official press, Libreria Pontificia, with a preface by the Secretary of State, Cardinal Gasparri. In it the author made the rather startling statement that, had the Camerlengo permitted the cardinals to use the *accesso*, Cardinal Rampolla would have been elected Pope on the second scrutiny. However, the author cites no evidence to support this contention.[37]

The ballots

Voting in a papal election is a slow, solemn ritual, with each ballot taking between sixty and ninety minutes. Only the cardinal-electors are allowed in the Sistine Chapel when a vote is taken. The junior cardinal-deacon is responsible for ensuring that all doors are locked for the duration of a ballot. Immediately after the cardinals have invoked the Holy Spirit the first vote is to be taken. The Constitution gives the most precise instructions about the conduct of a ballot. If the first vote is on the afternoon of the first day, no further vote is taken on that day. On subsequent days, however, four ballots are permitted, two in the morning and two in the afternoon. There is to be a drawing of lots to form teams of three cardinals to perform specific functions within the conclave: the scrutineers, to sort and count the votes; the revisers, to check the accuracy of the count; and the *infirmarii*, to collect the votes of any cardinals who may be confined to their beds. These teams are to be changed every three days, also by the drawing of lots.

All cardinal-electors must vote in each ballot. The voting paper must be rectangular in shape. It must have in the centre upper-half the inscription *Eligo in summum pontificem* ('I elect as Supreme Pontiff'). Each cardinal must complete the paper in secret. He writes the name of his choice, and nothing else, using handwriting that so far as possible cannot be identified as his. Two different names on the paper would spoil that vote, but would not invalidate the whole ballot. The paper should be folded twice.

Having completed their ballot papers they, individually and in order of seniority, approach the altar, holding their papers up so that they can clearly be seen. They kneel at the altar, pray for a short time and then rise to pronounce the following oath: "*I call as my witness Christ the Lord who will be my judge, that my vote is given to the one who before God I consider should be elected.*" This oath is taken only at the first ballot. The cardinals then place the ballot paper on a plate and drop it into a receptacle, bow to the altar and return to their places.

The three cardinals deputed to collect the votes from those confined to their rooms take with them a box with an opening on top for the ballot paper to be inserted. Before they leave the Sistine Chapel the scrutineers will open the box to show the cardinals that it is empty. The box is then locked and the key placed on the altar. When they return to the Chapel the box is opened by the scrutineers to ensure that the number of ballot papers in it corresponds to the number of cardinals confined to their rooms.

The counting of votes is conducted in full view of the cardinals. After the receptacle has been shaken to ensure the papers are mixed, one of the scrutineers takes them out. They are counted and if the number of papers does not correspond to the number of electors, the ballot is declared void. The voting papers must all be burned and a second ballot taken immediately. If the numbers are in agreement, the first scrutineer unfolds each ballot and notes the name before passing it to a second scrutineer. He also notes the name and passes it to the third scrutineer who reads the name aloud and then pierces the ballot with a threaded needle. If, on opening a ballot paper, a scrutineer should find a second paper within it, the vote is counted as one if the name is the same on each, but if the names are different both votes are invalid. When the scrutineers have added up all the votes the three revisers check both the accuracy of the count and any notes made by the scrutineers, to ensure that their task has been carried out exactly and faithfully. If everything is in order, the result of the ballot is then officially declared.

Before the cardinals leave the Sistine Chapel all ballot papers must be burned. If, however, a second ballot follows immediately the papers of both ballots are burned together. The famous smoke from the chimney on the roof of the Sistine Chapel gives the first indication to the world outside whether or not a new pope has been elected. The smoke is created by burning the voting papers with dry straw to produce white smoke for a decisive ballot, with wet straw producing black smoke for indecisive ballots. Because false smoke signals confused the waiting public in past conclaves a chemical is now added to the straw to ensure a definite black or white.

The Constitution provides for cardinal-electors to record the votes, but at the end of each session they must surrender any notes about the voting and these are burned, together with the ballot papers. The only voting record permitted is a formal document drawn up by the Camerlengo at the end of the conclave. This document, detailing the result of each ballot, is put in a sealed envelope and placed in the Vatican Archives and may be opened by no one unless the Pope gives explicit permission.

If no one is elected after three days voting is to be suspended for a day for prayer, informal discussion among the cardinals and a brief spiritual exhortation by the senior cardinal-deacon. Voting then resumes for another seven ballots when, if there is still no outcome, there is to be a further pause for prayer, discussion and another exhortation by the senior cardinal-priest. Another series of seven ballots then follow before another pause for further discussion and an exhortation, this time by the senior cardinal-bishop. A third series of seven ballots then follows. By this stage, if there is still no conclusion, the cardinals will have spent at least eight days in conclave and cast 30 ballots. The Camerlengo will ask the cardinals to vote on whether they wish to adopt an alternative method of election and, if so, which one? An absolute majority in favour of one or other alternative is necessary before either can be validly adopted.

Although the Constitution naturally provides for a long conclave recent papal elections have been relatively short. In 1800 the conclave lasted three months and in 1831, seven weeks. No conclave since then has even remotely approached their length. This can be clearly seen from the number of ballots required to elect each pope in the last ten conclaves:

1846	(Pius IX)	4
1878	(Leo XIII)	3
1903	(Pius X)	7
1914	(Benedict XV)	10
1922	(Pius XI)	14
1939	(Pius XII)	3
1958	(John XXIII)	11
1963	(Paul VI)	6
1978	(John Paul I)	4
1978	(John Paul II)	8

In terms of time, most of these conclaves lasted about four days. However, there were only two ballots each day in 1903, but in all subsequent elections there were four daily. The shortest conclave in modern history was in 1939, when it took only 25 hours and 40 minutes to elect Pope Pius XII (Cardinal Pacelli). The second shortest was first of the two conclaves of 1978, when it took 30 minutes longer for Cardinal Luciani (John Paul I) to reach the required majority.

8

The New Pope

The Constitution exhorts the person elected not to refuse the office for fear of its weight but to submit humbly to the design of divine will. "God who imposes the burden will sustain him with his hand, so that he will be able to bear it. In conferring the heavy task upon him, God will also help him to accomplish it and, in giving him the dignity, he will grant him the strength not to be overwhelmed by the weight of his office."

When one person receives the required majority the Cardinal-Dean or the senior cardinal-elector asks him in the name of the electoral college: "Do you accept your canonical election as Supreme Pontiff?" He becomes Pope immediately on giving an affirmative reply. He is then asked by what name he wishes to be known. The Master of Ceremonies draws up a document certifying the acceptance of his election by the new Pope and the name he has chosen. It is an old custom, but not a regulation, that a pope takes the name of one of his predecessors. The last pope to choose an original name was Lando in 913. The 146 popes since then have used only 32 names. The only Pope in the last 600 years to choose his own name was Adrian VI, the Dutchman elected in 1522 and the last non-Italian Pope before 'Papa Woytyla'. John Paul I, by his choice, sought to honour the memory of his two immediate predecessors. He was the first pope to choose two names.

The Constitution states that if the person elected is not already a bishop he must immediately receive episcopal ordination from the Cardinal-Dean or the senior cardinal-bishop. The formal public announcement of the election is to be delayed until after the ordination. Apart from this stipulation, the Constitution gives no guidance on how the cardinals should proceed in the event of a person outside the conclave being elected. There is no modern precedent to go on, because it is well over 600 years since a non-cardinal became Pope. Presumably, he would have to be contacted and asked to come to the conclave straight away. Do they telephone him or send a cardinal to convey the news in person? In any event, the initial contact would have to be conducted very discreetly so as to provide an opportunity for him to prepare mentally, emotionally and spiritually. He would also need time and space to decide freely whether or not to accept his election.

Immediately after the new Pope accepts his election the cardinals signify their obedience to him. This is followed by an act of thanksgiving. The senior Cardinal-deacon goes to the balcony of the Hall of Benedictions to make the formal public announcement to the crowd in St Peter's Square. A short time later the new Pope appears on the balcony to give the apostolic blessing, *Urbi et Orbi*.

From the moment of his election the life of the new Pope is changed utterly. The distinctive white soutane that he will always wear in public from now on – adapted from the traditional habit of the Dominican order – seems to symbolise that profound alteration. When Pope John Paul II's election was formally announced to the cardinals in the conclave of October 1978, his close friend, the Polish journalist Jerzy Turowicz, said the new Pope was "as alone as a man can be."[38] Cardinal Basil Hume looked at him from across the Sistine Chapel when it was announced that he had reached the required majority. His face was buried in his hands. "I felt desperately sad for the man", Hume observed.[39] The new pope himself captured this sense of desolation when he described his situation as "a clear cut-off from one's previous life with no possibility of return."[40] Karol Woytyla's reaction was not untypical. Pope Leo XIII was appalled at the certainty of his own election in 1878, protesting his unsuitability and lack of competence to the conclave with great emotion: "I must address the Sacred College. I fear they are about to make a sad mistake."[41] Pope Paul VI thought the papacy "a terrible cross." Giuseppi Sarto, when it became clear that he was on the verge of election as Pius X, spoke to the conclave with trembling voice and tears: "My election will be the ruin of the Church. Forget me!" So passionate were his pleas that many of the cardinals felt his candidature could no longer be considered.[42] His friends among the cardinals had to plead with him not to withdraw his name. Pius X must have found the burden of the papacy an extremely difficult cross to bear, but he bore it with great fortitude nonetheless. He began his first encyclical with these words: "It matters not to tell with what tears we sought to avoid this appalling burden of the pontifical office."[43] In 1954 Sarto became St Pius X, the last Pope to be canonised. When the Camerlengo, Cardinal Jean Villot, put the formal question to Cardinal Luciani at the end of the first conclave in 1978, "Do you accept your canonical election of Supreme Pontiff?", he hesitated for a few moments and the question had to be repeated. With a sigh, Luciani eventually replied: "May God forgive you for what you have done in this regard. I accept."[44]

One of the few popes whose recorded thoughts on the day of his election have been made public is John XXIII. For two days the cardinals had been unable to make up their minds between Cardinal Roncalli, the Patriarch of Venice, and Cardinal Agaganian, an Armenian who had been attached to the Roman Curia for many years. On the third day, however, Roncalli began to pull away towards the 35 votes needed and by lunchtime his election was a foregone conclusion. It was achieved in the first vote of the afternoon with, it is believed, 38 votes. That night he recorded the following in his diary: "O Jesus, I too can say what Pope Pius XII said when he was elected: *Miserere mei, Deus, secundum magnam misericordiam tuam* ('Have mercy on me, O Lord, according to thy great mercy', Psalm 51). One would say that it was like a dream and yet, until I die, it is the most solemn reality of all my life."[45]

There is a striking calmness about this diary entry. Yet, when earlier that day the Dean of the College of Cardinals, Eugene Tisserant, asked him formally if he accepted his election as pope, Cardinal Roncalli replied 'Listening to your voice, *tremens factus sum et ego, et timeo* ('I tremble and am seized by fear').[46]

Only a person totally unsuitable for the office could entertain a personal ambition for the papacy today, so awesome are its responsibilities. The formal catalogue of titles the new pope inherits serves to emphasise the burden of the office:

Vicar of Christ, a title dating from about the eighth century, which expresses the Pope's claim to universal jurisdiction. It derives from Christ's appointment of Peter as leader and shepherd of the whole Church (Mt 16:18-19), thus leaving him the visible representative, or vicar, of Christ on earth; Pope Innocent III (1160-1216) was the first pope to employ the title 'Vicar of Christ' regularly.

Successor to the Chief of the Apostles: The Pope is in apostolic succession to St Peter;

Supreme Pontiff of the Universal Church: The term Pontiff – from the Latin *pontifex*, a combination to two words meaning 'bridgebuilder' – was used of bishops from the fourth century. The chief bishop, the Pope, became known as *Pontifex Maximus,* Supreme Pontiff;

Patriarch of the West: A title dating from the sixth century indicating the Bishop of Rome's supreme jurisdiction over Western Christendom. The East has four historic patriarchates – Alexandria, Constantinople, Antioch and Jerusalem;

Primate of Italy: A title that recognises Rome as the *prima sedes* (principal see) of Italy;

Archbishop and Metropolitan of the Roman Province: Though known as the 'Bishop' of Rome, the Pope is in fact an archbishop and the presiding prelate (metropolitan) of the dioceses within the ecclesiastical province of Rome;

Sovereign of Vatican City State: The Pope is temporal ruler of Vatican City, the tiny (108-acre) independent state in west Rome, recognised as sovereign territory since the Lateran Treaty of 1929 between Italy and the Holy See. The Treaty "finally and irrevocably" settled the 'Roman Question' that had bedevilled relations between Italy and the Holy See since 1870 when the State took over Rome and declared the city to be its capital. Vatican City is all that now remains of the Papal States, once the largest concentrations of landed property in Italy. The Papal States had their origin in the edict of Constantine in 321, which declared the Church capable of holding property. The most important use to which the incomes derived from these lands was put was the provisioning of the city of Rome and feeding the proletariat. As one historian of the Papal States wrote, "the Pope possessed something between an immense soup kitchen and a public ministry of supply."[47] However, the Papal States meant the popes were frequently in controversy over territory and this did little to enhance their spiritual authority. Their loss was a blessing in disguise for it greatly increased the moral authority of the papal office. One historian, reviewing the history of the twentieth century, wrote that "...the nineteenth century liberation of the papacy (which sometimes seemed the most threatened of all religious institutions) from its responsibility for the government of large areas of Italy made it possible for Roman Catholics to feel uncompromising loyalty towards it."[48] Another felt that, "a big part of the rise in the Pope's authority as a churchman was connected with the collapse of his authority as a politician."[49] The Pope's temporal authority was reduced in the Lateran Treaty to what author George Bull called "the lace handkerchief dimensions" of Vatican City State.[50] Nevertheless, its independence guarantees the Pope liberty of action. As one author remarked, "the indispensable condition making it possible for the Vicar of Christ to be truly free and independent in the exercise of his office, consists in the full sovereignty and dominion of the Holy See over a piece of territory, however small."[51] Pope John Paul II told the United Nations General Assembly in 1979: "The territorial extent of that (Holy See) sovereignty is limited to the small state of Vatican City, but the sovereignty is warranted by the need of the Papacy to exercise its mission in full freedom, and to be able to deal with any interlocutor, whether a government or an international organisation, without dependence on other sovereignties." [52]

Servant of the Servants of God.

It is the last of the formal titles, 'Servant of the Servants of God', that resonated most with Albino Luciani and Karol Woytyla after their election. Pope John Paul I dispensed with the ceremonial coronation that traditionally marked the beginning of a new pontificate. There would be no tiara to signify the regal splendour of the papacy that belonged to another age. The formal ceremony of inauguration was to be much simpler than was customary up to then, when popes were crowned with the tiara and carried on a portable chair (called the *sedia gestatoria*), accompanied by acolytes bearing ostrich plumes. John Paul II followed his predecessor's example seven weeks later. He insisted that the formal ceremony marking the beginning of his pontificate on Sunday 22 October 1978 would be a Mass in St Peter's Square, to be described simply as "the solemn initiation of his ministry as Pastor of the Universal Church."

It is strange that among all the appellations listed above the word 'Pope' – Latin *papa*, 'father' – is not among them, yet that is the title by which he is universally known. In ancient times the title was given to bishops in the Western Church. In the East it was widely used in monastic communities and became the usual title for priests in the Orthodox Churches, like 'Father' in the Anglicised West. The term 'Pope' was gradually restricted in the Western Church from the middle of the sixth century. At the

Synod of Pavia in 998 the Archbishop of Milan was rebuked for using it of himself. The matter was formally settled in 1073 when Pope Gregory VII prohibited its use by any bishop other than the Bishop of Rome.

The inauguration of the ministry of the new Pope is normally held in St Peter's Square on the Sunday following his election. Sometime later the Pope takes ceremonial possession of St John Lateran's, the cathedral of Rome diocese. That is the day, in the magnificent setting of *la nostra basilica* in Piazza San Giovanni, when the people of Rome get the opportunity to welcome their new bishop home.

NOTES

1. George Schweiger in 'Pope', *Encyclopedia of Theology*; London 1975.
2. St Irenaeus, *Against Heresies*, Book 3, Chapter 2, Line 2, in *Early Christian Fathers*, Cyril Richardson (ed.), p.371; New York, 1970.
3. Apostolic Constitution of Pope Paul VI, *Romano Pontificio Eligendo*, introduction; Vatican City, 1975.
4. Apostolic Constitution of Pope John Paul II, *Universi Dominici Gregis*, introduction; Vatican City, 1996.
5. Horace K. Mann, *The Lives of the Popes in the Middle Ages*. vol x, p.16; London, 1925.
6. *ibid.* at footnote 6, p.14, where the author cites contemporary authorities to show "how preposterous it is to suppose that the anti-imperial majority (ie, supporters of Alexander) would bind themselves to the observance of a condition which would have rendered the election of a Pope a moral impossibility under the circumstances."
7. *ibid.*, p.140.
8. Paul VI, *Romano Pontificio Eligendo*, introduction.
9. *ibid.*, par.33.
10. Quoted in Owen Chadwick, *History of the Popes, 1830-1914*, p.4; Oxford, 1998.
11. Andrew M. Greeley, *The Making of the Popes*, p.277; London 1979.
12. Owen Chadwick, *History of the Popes*, 1830-1914.
13. Biography of Leo XIII, the Papal Library; www.vatican.va
14. Alan Palmer, *Metternich, Counsellor Europe*, p.294; London 1972.
15. Geoffrey Barraclough, *The Medieval Papacy*, p.161; London 1968.
16. Joannes Sagmuller, 'Exclusion, Right of' in *Catholic Encyclopedia,* vol v; New York, 1911.
17. Friedrich Engel-Janosi, 'l'Autriche au Conclave de 1903', in *Revue Belge de Philologie et d'Histoire*, vol xxix, 1951, pp.1119-1141.
18. Philip Hughes, *Short History of the Catholic Church,* p.239; London, 1974.
19. *ibid.*

20. *ibid*. Engel-Janosi's article cites a letter dated November 1904 in which a Vatican diplomatic representative said he was told by the Greek Rite Archbishop of Lemberg (modern Lviv) that Puzyna, a close friend, had confided to him that he was the instigator of the veto. See also footnote p.382 in *History of the Catholic Church* (ed. Hubert Jedin and John Dolan), London, 1983, where Puzyna is quoted as saying: "Austria did not use me; I used Austria."

21. John T. Ellis, *Life of James Cardinal Gibbons, Archbishop of Baltimore*, pp.353-4; Milwaukee, 1952.

22. Cardinal F.D. Mathieu, 'Les Dernier Jours de Leon XIII et le Conclave de 1903', in *Revue Des Deus Monde*, tome vingtieme, pp.242-285; Paris, 1 March 1904.

23. *ibid*.

24. *History of the Church* (ed, Hubert Jedin and John Dolan), vol ix, p.381; London, 1983.

25. 'Les Derniers Jours...', ref. note 19 above.

26. Cardinal Merry del Val, *Memories of Pope Pius X*, p.1; London, 1939.

27. 'Les Derniers Jours...', ref. note 19 above.

28. Pius X Apostolic Constitution, *Vacante Sede Apostolica*, par.79; Vatican City, 25 December 1904.

29. Pius X decree, *Commissum Nobis,* 25 January 1904.

30. Logue to Archbishop W. Walsh of Dublin, 9 August 1903; Walsh Papers, Dublin Diocesan Archives.

31. Engel-Janosi, 'l'Autriche au Conclave de 1903', p.1137, refers to a letter from Kopp to German Chancellor von Bulow, dated 4 Aug 1903, in which he informed the Chancellor of his approach to Rampolla.

32. Paul VI, *Romano Pontificio Eligendo*, par.79.

33. Pius X, Apostolic Constitution, *Vacante Sede Apostolica.*

34. Pius XII, Apostolic Constitution, *Vacantis Apostolicae Sedis;* Vatican City, 8 December 1945.

35. 'Les Derniers Jours...'

36. Pius X, Apostolic Constitution, *Vacante Sede Apostolica,* 25 December 1904.

37. Monsignor Pietro Sinopoli di Giunti, *Il Cardinale Mariano Rampolla del Tindaro,* at p.214: *'Se il Cardinale Oreglia avesse permesso il diritto di accesso, il Cardinale Mariano Rampolla sarebbe stato proclamato Papa al secondo scrutinio'*; Vatican City, 1923.

38. Quoted in George Weigel, *Witness to Hope: A Biography of Pope John Paul II*, p.254; Cliff Street Books, 1999.
39. *ibid.*
40. *ibid.*
41. O'Reilly, *Life of Leo XIII*, p.310, quoted in Allen S. Will, *Life of James Cardinal Gibbons*, p.315; Baltimore, 1911.
42. Eye-witness account by Cardinal James Gibbons, quoted by J.T.Ellis in his biography, *James Cardinal Gibbons*; Milwaukee, 1952.
43. Pius X, encyclical letter *E Supremi Apostolus*, 4 October 1903.
44. These words were borrowed from St Bernard of Clairvaux who uttered them when he heard that one of his monks had been elected Pope; quoted by Andrew Greeley in *The Making of the Popes*, p.154; London, 1979.
45. *Vent'Anni dalla Elezione di Giovanni XXIII*, diary of Pope John XXIII, p.12, Loris Capovilla (ed), Rome, 1978. Quoted by Peter Hebblethwaite in *John XXIII: Pope of the Council*, p.284; London 1984.
46. *ibid.*, Capovilla, p.50, Hebblethwaite, p.285.
47. Peter Partner, *The Lands of St Peter: The Papal States in the Middle Ages and the Early Renaissance*, pp.6-9; London, 1972.
48. J.M. Roberts, *The Penguin History of the Twentieth Century*, p.168; London, 1999.
49. Owen Chadwick, *A History of the Popes, 1830-1914*, p.247; Oxford, 1998.
50. George Bull, *Inside the Vatican*, p.127; London, 1982.
51. Rene Fulop-Miller, *The Power and Secret of the Vatican*; London, 1935.
52. John Paul II, address to the U.N. General Assembly, 2 October 1979.